POWER BASICS OF
BASKETBALL

James Bryce
Bill Polick

Prentice-Hall, Inc.
Englewood Cliffs, New Jersey

Prentice-Hall International, Inc., *London*
Prentice-Hall of Australia, Pty. Ltd., *Sydney*
Prentice-Hall Canada Inc., *Toronto*
Prentice Hall of India Private Ltd., *New Delhi*
Prentice-Hall of Japan, Inc., *Toyko*
Prentice-Hall of Southeast Asia Pte. Ltd., *Singapore*
Whitehall Books, Ltd., *Wellington, New Zealand*
Editora Prentice-Hall do Brasil, Ltda., *Rio de Janeiro*
Prentice-Hall Hispanoamericana, S.A., *Mexico*

© 1985 by
James Bryce
Bill Polick

Library of Congress Cataloging in Publication Data

Bryce, James
  Power basics of basketball.

  Summary: Text and photos present instructions in
playing basketball, and some outstanding players
present their own pointers and philosophy of the game.
  1. Basketball—Juvenile literature.   2. Walton,
Bill—Juvenile literature.   3. Hazzard,
Walt—Juvenile literature.   4. Lee, Greg—Juvenile
literature.   [1. Basketball]   I. Polick, Bill,
    II. Title.
GV885.5.B79   1985   796.32'32   84-18342

ISBN 0-13-688300-1

Printed in the United States of America

The Early Beginnings

Basketball, like no other major sport, is an original of the United States. Its origins are not embedded in ancient history, as are those of most other sports.

For all its worldwide popularity, basketball was founded less than one hundred years ago (1891) in Springfield, Massachusetts, by a young doctor of physical education, James Naismith.

Naismith was teaching physical education at the Young Men's Christian Association (YMCA) College in Springfield and was given the dubious job of keeping the students physically fit and pleasantly occupied during the long, boring winter days that can hang over the Northeast.

Naismith realized that he needed to keep his sometimes rebellious students active and interested in some form of sports activity while keeping them indoors away from the near-freezing cold of the Massachusetts winter.

He originally tried a form of indoor rugby, but the rough tackles and blocks were simply too bone-jarring on a gym floor. In trying to adapt soccer as an indoor game, he soon realized that the confined area produced more broken windows (and broken arms) than enjoyable recreation.

Frustrated, Naismith decided he would not try to adapt any other existing game but instead would develop a new sports contest that would work within the confines of the gym.

His idea was to develop a game requiring skill over brute strength. Thus his choice of a ball and an elevated basket met his requirement exceptionally well.

Moving his players back and forth along the gym floor, passing the ball and then having to elevate it into the basket proved all his concepts. The game provided the students with the exercise they needed; it required the students to develop skills for hand, eye, and body coordination; and, most important of all, the students enjoyed the new game with a passion that surprised Naismith beyond his wildest expectations.

Naismith's first basketball was actually a soccer ball, and his basket was indeed just that—a pair of peach baskets mounted ten feet above the floor at each end of the YMCA gym.

It was in early 1892 that Naismith's thirteen rules were first published in the school paper. It is said that Naismith insisted that the game be called what it was—basketball.

The name and the game caught on, and soon competitive team play between rival YMCA clubs and colleges swept across the country. Professional clubs followed, and today the National Basketball Association (NBA) and the National College Athletic Association (NCAA) bring basketball to those people wanting to play the game and to those millions of sports fans who love to watch this fantastic sporting event.

Basketball's popularity in the last fifty years has spread to Canada, to Europe, and to South America. It has become a major spectator sport the world over, with fans in almost every country.

James Naismith might not recognize the modern basket hoop in comparison to his old peach baskets, but he would be very pleased with what his game has achieved and with the enjoyment he has brought to so many people.

Each summer some of the biggest names in basketball pack their uniforms and head out on the road once again to move across a gym floor, passing, dribbling, and shooting the ball into the hoop suspended ten feet above them.

No, it's not some new summer league, and the players and coaches will be back playing or coaching with the NBA or their respective colleges come September. But for this summer, as for so many other summers, they are on their way to teach at various summer basketball camps.

Bill Walton, Walt Hazzard, Greg Lee, and scores of other basketball greats will crisscross the country, teaching the game and giving one-on-one tips to those fortunate few who can make it into the limited summer camp rosters.

The cost of most summer camps is not prohibitive and is worth every cent one might have to pay.

But even if the camps were free, the limited enrollment (usually sixty to seventy kids) still cannot begin to handle the thousands of young people wanting the opportunity to learn from the very best. Recognizing this limitation prompted the concept for the *Power Basics of Sports* (Basketball).

The concept was easily stated: "Let's find a way for all the future basketballers to acquire that same one-on-one type of basic basketball teaching directly from those athletes and coaches who put on the summer training camps."

Indeed, the concept was clearly understood; it was the method of doing it that took some working out.

But the challenge was met, and soon there were TV crews and still photographers moving about a high school basketball floor, taking rolls of videotape and hundreds and hundreds of photographs of three of America's finest basketball players: Bill Walton, Walt Hazzard, and Greg Lee. (More about them later.)

And when the TV cameras stopped and the still camera shutters fell for the last time, it was apparent that everyone had done a superb job and that we had learned two important things: one, we had a very large amount of exciting videotape that could be made into an exceptional "how to" basketball instructional series; and two, we had an equally large amount of still action photos that could become an excellent "how to" instructional basketball book.

So, the *Power Basics of Sports* (Basketball) in both book and videocassette was brought into being to try to give the basketballer a one-on-one feel for the instructional material. Much of the dialogue you will read in this book is in the exact words of Bill Walton, Greg Lee, or Walt Hazzard as they were giving pointers, teaching a particular skill, or philosophizing about how they play the game.

Power Basics of Sports (Basketball) is just what it states: "A strong primer for the beginner and a solid reeducation program for those young people wanting to become even better."

The Cast

Bill Walton

Walt Hazzard

Greg Lee

Before giving you background on the trio of athletes in our program, we would like to explain why we picked the three people we did.

Now, as in the past, one of the finest basketball teams in the country is UCLA (University of California at Los Angeles). Each year UCLA produces solid winning teams and many outstanding players.

In the recent past, however, UCLA was *the* most dominant team in the country year after year. Almost every conference or national championship came to them from the moment they appeared on any court, at home or on the road. They were consistently the All-American team, and from one coast to the other UCLA became the ultimate challenge in basketball.

The responsibility for developing these powerhouse teams fell on the shoulders of one man—Coach John Wooden. One of the most revered men in the game of basketball (both as player and as coach), John Wooden set the pace for all others to match. Only history will tell if anyone ever will. Below is a brief summary of his accomplishments (from the *Encyclopedia of Basketball*—Knopf 1977).

JOHN WOODEN

The record acknowledges scholarly and soft-spoken John Wooden as a coaching great. He has won eight NCAA championships in a nine-year span, and in a 36-year career as a high school and college coach, Wooden's teams have won almost 80 percent of their games and never had a losing season. Through 1972 he had won 583 games and lost only 154, and was fifth on the all-time winning list. Wooden is another exponent of deliberate basketball. His teams are characterized by conditioning, fundamentals of speed, quickness and basketball sense, which Wooden describes as "the ability to be in the right place at the right time." Wooden was voted into the Hall of Fame as a player in 1960 and as a coach in 1972, the only man to be twice-honored by the Hall of Fame.

In forming our ideas for the *Power Basics of Sports* (Basketball), we felt we needed to start with those strong fundamentals that still hold up year after year. What better way to do that than by using those athletes who were coached with the John Wooden method and who have gone on to capitalize on that method and expand it into their very own self-expression as professional players or coaches.

The three players we have chosen were each All-Americans under Coach John Wooden, and they are still contributing to basketball as a major part of their lives.

BILL WALTON

(Player–Instructor)

Regarded by peers, press, and fans as one of the all-time best centers in basketball, Bill is currently the center for the Los Angeles Clippers.

At UCLA, Bill was a unanimous All-American selection for three straight years, averaging 20.3 points per game and 15.7 rebounds.

As an NBA pro-star, Bill led the Portland Trailblazers to an NBA title and has been named the NBA's Most Valuable Player.

In addition to covering center for the Clippers, Bill has recently completed his third year of law school.

WALT HAZZARD

(Coach)

As a player for UCLA, Walt Hazzard was a two-time All-American and was named by the U.S. Basketball Writers Association as player of the year (1964). In that same year, he led the U.S. Olympic team to a gold medal.

As a ten-year superstar of the NBA, he played in over 720 games, with a 12.6 average per game.

Walt has been head coach of Compton College (53–9) and Chapman College (44–14). Walt is now the head coach at UCLA.

GREG LEE
(Instructor)

Greg Lee was a high school All-American for two straight years and then went on to play for John Wooden (with coplayer Bill Walton) at UCLA. Greg was a three-year Academic All-American.

As a professional (club player), Greg played in Europe with teams in West Germany. At present Greg is a coach in San Diego, California, and conducts basketball clinics across the country with partner Bill Walton.

In addition to their player or coaching duties, these three men teach hundreds of young people at summer basketball camps all across the country. Providing that same knowledge, skill, and energy to the *Power Basics of Sports* (Basketball), they open the way for any student of the game to develop into a better basketball player, a better athlete, and a better person.

Contents

POWER BASICS OF
BASKETBALL

1

Ball Handling

Greg Lee

Basketball has been a part of my life for many years. Through it I learned about self-worth and the sense of being part of a team. It's imperative that young people learn to play in the context of a group and get along with their teammates.

Basketball teaches you what is allowed and what isn't in the game, and that's something that carries over into everyday life. You learn self-discipline, and that creates better basketball teams and better citizens as well.

chapter 1

The Stance

The triple threat position is one of the most basic elements in basketball. It is used on both offense and defense and in almost every situation.

THE TRIPLE THREAT

Walt Hazzard

Basics, fundamentals, foundations. These are three words that describe the same thing: the elements on which a game is based.

For Bill, Greg, and me, the game is based on what we call the triple threat position. The triple comes from the three things you can do from the position: you can pass or receive a pass, you can dribble or drive, and you can shoot. On defense you can guard the man with the ball, guard the man without the ball, and break up plays.

The triple threat is simply a position for your body, and you should learn it before you go on to any other part of the game.

In Picture 1 you can see Bill demonstrating the proper position. Notice that his feet are shoulder-width apart and that his weight is on the balls of his feet, with his heels just slightly touching the floor. You can also see that he's bending slightly and dropping his hips. His head is centered between his feet and his chin is up. Notice also that he's keeping his hands above his waist.

Practice the triple threat position as much as possible. Because you will be using it so much, it should become second nature; you should not have to think about doing it.

Picture 1

Picture 2

THE JUMP STOP

Greg Lee

When you have mastered the triple threat position, you have to learn how to get into it during a game after running, rebounding, or making a play. You use what is called the jump stop, as in Picture 2.

Bill Walton

Imagine yourself running down the court to set up a play. You don't just stop running, then get into position; that would take extra time. The way to do it is with a jump stop.

Look at Picture 3, and you will see what I mean. The student has just finished a proper stop and is in the triple threat position.

Picture 3

In the jump stop, both feet hit the floor at the same time, as in Picture 4. Your weight goes right to the balls of your feet. Don't stop on your heels because your momentum will carry you forward, and you will not be able to move or pivot quickly. The jump stop keeps you from traveling with the ball and gives you a choice of pivot feet. If you land on one foot before the other, you are stuck and cannot pivot the other way. Maintain the triple threat position.

Once you have made your jump stop and are in the triple threat position, you have to learn how to pivot and turn. When you have the ball, you cannot pivot on one foot after you have used the other, so it is important to know when, and how, to do it properly.

Picture 4

PIVOT AND TURN

Walt Hazzard

There are two ways to pivot: to the inside and to the outside. The inside pivot means turning toward the basket or toward your opponent, as in Picture 5. The outside pivot means turning away from the basket or your opponent. Always pivot on the balls of your feet, never on the heels, or you will be off balance.

Picture 5

In Picture 6 I'm the opponent, and Bill is demonstrating the outside pivot. Notice how he is turning on the ball of his left foot and how he is maintaining his balance. It is important to learn not to lean with your head because that will throw you off balance.

If Bill had the ball and wanted to get around me, he would take a short step in one direction and then explode in the opposite direction.

Picture 6

Greg Lee

Be sure to plant your foot firmly, then push off in the other direction. This fake will make the defender think you are going one way, and he will be off balance. You gain the advantage because by the time the defender recovers, you are a step or two past him.

Always remember to use the triple threat position. To get into it, use a good jump stop. Maintain balance and pivot on the balls of your feet.

chapter 2

Dribbling

Dribbling is very important in the game of basketball. It is one of two ways of moving the ball around the court, and is one of the keys to a successful offense.

WHEN TO DRIBBLE

Walt Hazzard

As with so many things in basketball, dribbling begins with a good triple threat position, as in Picture 7. Master the triple threat, then learn to dribble.

Dribbling is probably the most misused element in the game. Too many times players will receive a pass and begin dribbling right away. Once you start to dribble, you are no longer in the triple threat position, and your alternatives are limited.

Bill Walton

The skills involved in dribbling are pretty simple. To begin, keep your elbow close to your body, as in Picture 8. This helps keep the ball close to your body and gives the defender less opportunity to steal the ball. If your elbow is out, the ball will be too, and the defensive player can reach between your body and the ball and swipe it away.

Just as in the triple threat position, keep your chin up when you dribble so that you can see the court, and you will

Picture 7

Picture 8

know what is going on around you. Keep your weight balanced on the balls of your feet.

Dribbling is not just bouncing the ball on the floor. It is "playing catch" with the floor. Don't bounce the ball too softly and don't slam it to the floor. Just develop a "touch" and control the ball.

Walt Hazzard

When you are dribbling the ball, be sure to keep your hand spread over the ball and don't touch it with the heel of your hand. You want to control it with your fingertips. In Picture 9 you see Greg dribbling properly. Notice that his elbow is close to his body, his head is up, and his fingertips are controlling the ball (Picture 10).

Picture 9

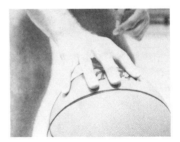

Picture 10

Dribble the ball about waist high for the best control. If you bounce the ball too high, the defender has a greater chance of stealing it away from you.

PROTECTING THE BALL

Greg Lee

Always remember to protect the ball with your body. If, for example, the defender is on your left, dribble the ball in your right hand and protect the ball with your left shoulder, arm, hip, and leg. If the defender is on your right, protect the ball with the right side of the body.

In Picture 11 you can see how I am blocking the ball with

Picture 11

the right side of my body and dribbling with my left hand. There is no way my opponent can reach in and steal the ball.

This leads to another important element of dribbling: You must be able to dribble the ball with either hand (Pictures 12 and 13). This gives you greater flexibility because you can keep the ball away from the defender no matter which side your opponent comes from.

Picture 12

Picture 13

Dribbling takes practice. Work on it in the gym, at home, on the playground, and practice with both hands to develop a "touch."

chapter 3

Passing

Passing is the second method of moving the ball around the court. There are two types of passes: the bounce pass and the chest pass.

THE CHEST PASS

Walt Hazzard

Imagine yourself in a game. You have the ball, your opponent has you blocked from the basket, and you are stuck. Your teammate breaks free from his defender and is on the way to the hoop. You snap a pass to him, and he drives in for a lay-up. The only reason the play worked is that your pass was well executed.

Passing is very important in the game of basketball, and passing well is a skill you must learn to succeed in.

There are several elements to use in both the chest pass and the bounce pass: Start in the triple threat position, spread your hands over the ball, as in Picture 14, so that you are controlling it with your fingertips, keep the ball under your chin, step toward the target, and try to put the ball where it can be received by your teammate. Greg demonstrates the proper position in Picture 15.

In Picture 16 you see Greg stepping toward his opponent as he is getting ready to release the ball. This is important because it helps you control the ball better.

When you pass the ball, snap your wrists so that the back of your hands face each other and your thumbs end up pointing at the floor (Picture 17). This puts a little reverse spin on the ball.

Picture 14

Picture 15

Picture 16

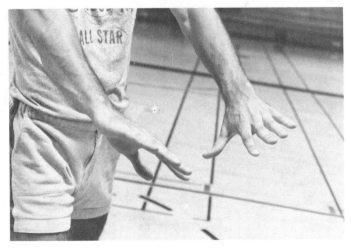

Picture 17

The chest pass is just what its name implies: a pass of the ball at chest level. When you pass the ball, aim directly at your teammate's upper body and remember that as the passer, it is your responsibility to make the play work.

When you are on the receiving end of a pass, remember to keep your hands up and ready. If the ball comes in on the right side of your body, you should block it with your right hand and tuck it with the left hand. If it is on the left side, block left and tuck right.

It is not always possible to pass the ball directly to your teammate, and that is where the bounce pass comes in.

THE BOUNCE PASS

Bill Walton

The bounce pass begins in the same way as the chest pass, but, instead of snapping it directly to your teammate, bounce it off the floor. You must put reverse spin on the ball, so

Picture 18

Picture 19

remember to snap your wrists and point your thumbs at the floor so that the ball doesn't jump off the floor. The ball should bounce about two-thirds of the way to the receiver and should come up at waist level.

Notice in Picture 18 that the student is bouncing the ball at the right spot, and in Picture 19 the ball is coming in to the receiver at the proper height.

To develop good passing skills, try playing a game we call "Monkey in the Middle."

MONKEY IN THE MIDDLE

Walt Hazzard

This game is a lot like "Keep Away." Get two other players. Put one player in the middle and have that person try to steal the ball as it is passed back and forth (Picture 20).

Picture 20

To make successful passes, you have to keep the defensive player guessing. Use a lot of fakes. Fake under and pass over your opponent or fake over and pass under. Don't lob the ball. Pass the ball by the defender or through him. One way to almost guarantee success is to pass the ball right by the opponent's ear. I promise the defensive player will move his head!

When you're playing "Monkey in the Middle," trade places several times so that you can practice defending the pass as well as passing. Use a lot of head and body fakes, and remember to use both the chest pass and the bounce pass. Picture 21 illustrates what I mean when I say pass through your opponent.

When you play a game like "Monkey in the Middle," remember that you can learn to play defense as well as offense when you are on the court.

Picture 21

chapter 4

Playing Against the Smaller, Faster Player

We tend to think of all basketball players as tall, but there are different degrees of tall! In almost every game, you will find yourself going against a defender who is bigger or smaller than you are, and you have to know how to handle the situation.

TAKING YOUR ADVANTAGE

Bill Walton

During the course of a basketball game, each player has to be able to execute certain plays to take advantage of mismatch situations. One of those is playing against an opponent who is smaller and faster than you are.

Your main goal is to get the ball to the hoop or to continue the play without letting the defender take advantage of his quickness by crowding you.

Once again, start with the triple threat position and keep your back to your opponent. Keep your elbows out when you have the ball, and keep your defender between your elbows. Look at Picture 22, and you will see what I mean. If the defender tries to reach around one side, you can easily drive, pass, or shoot the other way. Keep the defender close. If the defender moves off you, you have to close the distance to take advantage of your size and strength.

Work your way into the basket. use a lot of fakes so that your opponent doesn't know what you are going to do.

Picture 22

GET INTO POSITION

Greg Lee

It is important to get into position with a good two-footed stop. You have to maintain a wide base. Keep your elbows out because if they are too close to your body, the defender can control your position on the court (Picture 23). Keep your back to the defender. You cannot drive past him because he is quicker and can steal the ball.

Picture 23

Being bigger and slower than your opponent doesn't mean that you have to play roughly to counteract his speed. A little finesse goes a long way.

FAKE YOUR OPPONENT

Bill Walton

One way to get around your opponent, even though he is faster than you are, is to fake him out. Move left and right, and get your opponent doing the same. Then when he is leaning in

Picture 24

one direction, you can simply turn the other way and go right on past. The player in Picture 24 has done exactly that and is on his way for a shot.

It is very important to keep your opponent off balance. Keep him guessing. If you go one way consistently, he is going to be right with you. But if you vary your pattern, he will not know what to expect next, and when he leans in the wrong direction, you are gone!

chapter 5

A Special Power Basic

THE GIVE AND GO AND THE BACK DOOR CUT

Greg Lee

The give and go is one of the most effective plays in basketball. In this play you pass the ball to a teammate and then explode toward the basket (Diagram 1). You push off the

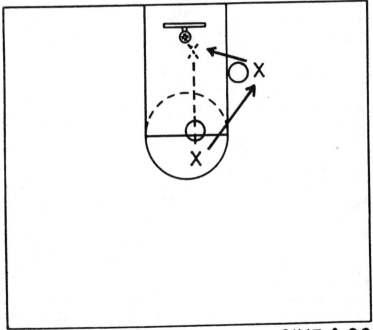

GIVE & GO

Diagram 1

outside foot at the instant you see that your defender is relaxed, and your teammate passes the ball back to you for the easy shot. You can use this play from any position on the floor, but timing is the key.

Another important play is called the back door cut. You move a step away from the basket, push off the outside foot, and cut in a straight line to the basket (Diagram 2). It is a very fast-action play, so it is important that you convert before the defense has a chance to react. Timing, once again, is the key. Don't make your cut too early or too late.

These two plays add extra dimensions to the game and will help you score more points.

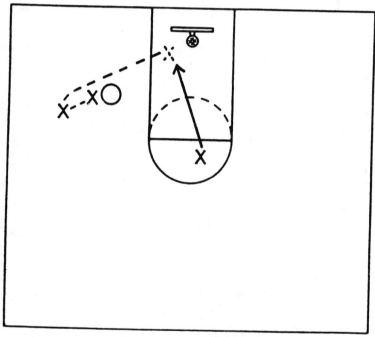

"BACK-DOOR CUT"

Diagram 2

chapter 6

A Power Basics Checklist

Use the triple threat position

Feet shoulder-width apart.

Bend at the knees.

Keep your head and chin up.

Hands above the waist.

Weight on the balls of the feet.

Head centered above feet.

Dribbling

Maintain the triple threat position.

Keep your eyes ahead.

Play catch with the floor.

Dribble ball close to body.

Protect ball with your body.

Passing

Step toward target.

Snap the wrists.

Keep palms of hands off the ball.

Bounce ball two-thirds of the way to target.

Put reverse spin on ball.

Playing against the smaller, faster player

Keep defender between elbows.

Stay close to opponent.

Don't face opponent.

Take advantage of your size.

2

Shooting

Walt Hazzard

Attaining success, whether it's in basketball or in life, means reaching a point of self-satisfaction, knowing you've done the best you possibly can.

Basketball is just a small part of life, but it can teach you lessons that will help you in the real world.

Through the game you learn that there is no substitute for hard work. You must give your all to achieve whatever goals you've set for yourself. To be a success, you must pay the price; to be the boss, you must pay the cost, and that means hard work.

chapter 7

Learning to Shoot

The object in the game of basketball is to win, and to do that you have to score points. Making a basket, especially in a critical situation, is one of the most rewarding experiences a player can have. But shooting well means mastering the techniques and having them instilled so deeply that they are automatic.

SET SHOT

Bill Walton

I have been playing basketball almost all my life, and I know that it takes a lot of hard work to reach the top. But you don't just absorb all the skills at once; you have to break them down into basic elements and practice them individually. That is especially true with shooting.

As you might expect, shooting begins with a good triple threat position. You should keep your head up so that you can see what is going on around you. Hold the ball right under your chin and keep your elbows close to your body, pointed at the floor. Cock your wrist. Look at Picture 25, and you will see Greg in the perfect position.

Shots don't begin in the hands or arms; they start with the legs. Bend your knees slightly, coil yourself as if you are ready to spring. Take a look at Picture 26. Notice how Greg is ready to spring up and shoot.

When you are in position, go straight up, not to the side, front, or back. Release the ball at the top of your movement, and follow through with your hand and arm as if they were

Picture 25

Picture 26

following the ball through the hoop. The index finger on your shooting hand should be the last thing that touches the ball.

In Picture 27 Greg shows the proper position. You'll notice that in all the pictures, he has his shoulders square with the basket. This allows him to aim the ball and control the shot. You can also see that he has the seams of the ball sideways so that his hand goes across them and not with them. This will give the ball the proper rotation.

Picture 27

Remember not to fade or lean away from the basket. The set shot is the first one you should master. It is the basic shot in the game and the stepping-stone for the more sophisticated shots.

Walt Hazzard

If you are a right-handed shooter, your right hand supports the ball. Keep the ball on your fingertips and don't let your palm touch the ball. Your left hand merely supports the ball and keeps it from falling as in Picture 28.

Picture 28

When you shoot the set shot, your feet should remain on the floor. You go down, then straight up to release the ball, and follow through as if you are reaching up and over the rim of the basket. If anything, you should lean a little forward as if you are going in behind the shot.

Once you have mastered the set shot and the fundamentals of shooting, you are ready to move on to the more advanced shots.

chapter 8

Other Types of Shots

You need a variety of shots to score in the game of basketball.
The set shot is one you will need, but it will not always work,
so it is important to master more sophisticated maneuvers.

THE JUMP SHOT

Walt Hazzard

Once you have mastered the fundamentals of shooting,
you can move on. The next shot to learn is the jump shot. It
begins the same way as a set shot: You maintain the triple
threat position, coil, and spring. There is one major difference,
however.

In Picture 29 Bill demonstrates the jump shot. The obvious
difference between this and the set shot is that you leap off the
floor as you shoot. This gives you several advantages: You
have a straighter shot at the basket, you are higher and have a
better view of the hoop, and you can possibly catch your
defender off guard. For maximum advantage, release the ball
at the top of your jump.

Greg Lee

When you use the jump shot, it is always a good idea to
do one or two fakes before you actually take the shot. This
helps confuse your opponent and throws his timing off so that
he doesn't know exactly when or if you are going to shoot. It
really gives you an advantage.

Picture 29

THE BANK SHOT

Bill Walton

Since you cannot always shoot directly at the hoop, you need to learn the bank shot. It is made from either side of the basket and is exactly what it sounds like: a shot where the ball is banked off the backboard and into the basket.

In Picture 30 you will see a small square on the backboard, just above the hoop. When you shoot the bank shot, aim for the side of that square on the side from which you are shooting. Aim about six inches above the rim. If the ball hits

Picture 30

Picture 31

this spot with the right rotation and speed, the ball should go into the basket.

You can use the bank shot as part of a set, jump, lay-up, or hook. Practice with each hand so that you can hit the spot as often as possible. In Picture 31 you see a student demonstrating the bank shot.

LAY-UP

Walt Hazzard

In a game you may sometimes find yourself dribbling toward the basket and discover that there are no defenders in your way. That is the time for the lay-up.

This shot involves driving toward the goal, pushing off on the foot opposite from the hand you are shooting with, and laying the ball on the backboard at the proper angle to fall into the net. In Picture 32 you see Bill as he approaches the basket. Picture 33 illustrates the foot and hand coordination, and in

Picture 32

Picture 33

Picture 34 he lays the ball on the backboard. It is very important to practice this shot from both sides. Get used to shooting with either hand, as Bill illustrates in Picture 35. You never know which side you will be coming in on.

It is very important to get the right feel for every shot. That is called the "touch." Practice shooting the different shots from various places on the court and practice with each hand because the defender will usually try to guard your stronger side. The more able you are to shoot from either hand, the better are your offensive weapons, and the more likely you are to score.

Picture 34

Picture 35

chapter 9

The Block and Roll (Offense)

Block and roll is not a new music form; it is an offensive maneuver that will help you score points in a basketball game.

USING YOUR TEAMMATES

Greg Lee

Many times on a basketball court, you are confronted with a defensive player who is making it hard for you to get your shot off; therefore, you want to use your teammates to help you get free to take a shot. That is where the block and roll comes in.

The play is one of the basics in the game. You use a player on your team to provide you with a screen.

SETTING THE SCREEN

Bill Walton

The most important thing in setting a screen is to screen the player, not the position. Since defenders are free to move, the person setting the screen has to be flexible enough to move with the opponent.

To set the screen, move in and make a good two-footed stop and protect yourself. In Picture 36 you see the beginning of a block and roll play. The player with the ball is blocked and calls for his teammate to set the screen. Picture 37 illustrates the screen in position.

Picture 36

Picture 37

When you are setting the screen, make sure the defender's shoulder hits you in the middle of the chest, as in Picture 38. This is the only way to keep him from getting

Picture 38

around you. Protect yourself in the groin area and chest with your arms. When your teammate with the ball comes beyond the defender, you should roll, or pivot, and open yourself up to the ball.

At that point your teammate with the ball has two options: to drive in for the shot or to pass the ball to you for the shot if you have a better opportunity. If you roll properly and your teammate shoots and misses, you should be in good position for the rebound.

Picture 39 shows how the screen effectively blocks out the defenders, and the player with the ball is able to make the play.

Picture 39

USING THE FAKE

Greg Lee

In order for the play to work, the player with the ball has to make a fake to convince the defender that he is going in one direction. This gives the other offensive player the opportunity to move into position. If the defender doesn't come back with you, you can go right past him.

Always remember to go with the play. Take advantage of your opponent's mistakes.

chapter 10

The Block and Roll (Defense)

How many times have you been to a basketball game and heard one of the defensive players yell "Switch!"? What the player is doing is communicating with a teammate and setting up the defense to the block and roll.

COMMUNICATION

Bill Walton

The most important element in good defense is communication between players. You have to let your teammates know where you are, what you are doing, and where your opponent is.

After the offense sets the screen, the defender who is guarding the player with the ball yells "Switch!" which means that the defensive players change the person they are guarding.

When you switch, make sure you jump out and attack the ball. Remember that these plays happen very quickly, and it is important for you to react as quickly as you possibly can.

Picture 40 shows the switch in progress. Just as the player with the ball starts to move out, the defender makes a call. In Picture 41 you see the other defender move out to the ball.

In this situation it is very important to slow down the offensive player as much as possible to keep that player from driving in toward the basket and getting a shot. You cannot just drop back and let the player have a chance to shoot.

Picture 40

Picture 41

Greg Lee

When you are guarding the player with the ball and the
offense screens you, try to make every effort to get through the

screen. Step out with your lead leg, throw your arm and shoulder out to try to get past the screen. If the screen is so well set that you cannot get through, then it is time to yell "Switch!"

WATCH THE FOULS

Walt Hazzard

In a tight situation like a block and roll, with four players or more in a very small area, it is important that you not foul anyone. Be aggressive, but not overly so. Play fairly and do your best.

chapter 11

A Special Power Basic

DEVELOPING A GOOD HOOK SHOT

Bill Walton

Learning to shoot the hook shot takes a lot of practice because it is the most difficult shot in the game. Start out by staying very close to the basket, then move from one side to the other as you shoot. Practice with each hand so that you get the feel of the ball. Use the backboard. Gradually work your way out from the basket.

Keep practicing. The more you work on this shot, the better you will be when it is time to use it in the game.

chapter 12

A Power Basics Checklist

Offense/shooting

Use the triple threat position.
Keep elbow close to the body, pointing to the floor.
Shot starts in the legs.
Follow through.
On jump shots, release ball at top of jump.
Aim ball at side of backboard square six inches above
rim.

Lay-ups and hook shots

Plant foot, go straight up.
Lay ball on backboard.
Hook shots start with jump stop, turn, step toward basket.
Reach into the basket on follow through.

Block and roll

Set screen on player, not the position.
Open up to follow play.
Fake opposite way to set screen.

Defending the block and roll

Communicate.
Switch the player you are guarding.
Jump to get new player.

3

The Complete Player

Bill Walton

Basketball is a fifty–fifty game. It is half offense, half defense and if you're not on one, you're on the other. The team that controls a game is the one that controls the backboards, gets both the offensive and defensive rebounds, and converts them into points.

Not everything you do on the court brings applause; some jobs are done without fanfare. That's the way life is off the court as well.

chapter 13

Rebounding

One of the most important elements that determines whether a team wins or loses a game is how well it controls the boards, how well it rebounds.

GETTING INTO POSITION

Greg Lee

A good rebound may not bring a huge cheer from the crowd, but it can certainly make the difference in a game. Having the ability to make rebounds makes you a more valuable player and gives your team an edge, but in order to retrieve the missed shot, you must practice the basics (Picture 42).

When you are moving in to the boards as a shot is being made, whether you are on offense or defense, one of the most important things to do is to assume that the shot will be missed. You have to be ready for any bounce the ball might take. In Picture 43 you see Bill in the ready position. Notice that as the ball approaches the basket, he has his eyes on the ball, and he is standing away from the hoop, not directly under it.

Always start a rebound away from the basket and move in when you see which direction the ball is going. Don't trap yourself underneath the hoop and watch the ball go bouncing off behind you. Seventy to 80 percent of the rebounds in a game are taken on the opposite side of the basket from the shot, so you should always be prepared to move in that direction.

Picture 42

Picture 43

TAKING THE BALL

Walt Hazzard

Once you have determined where the ball is going, move to that area and be ready. As the ball comes off the backboard, leap straight up for the ball. Be sure to keep a wide base and keep your elbows up. In Picture 44 you see Bill going up for the rebound. Notice that he is reaching up to catch the ball with both hands. That is the way to control the ball. Always catch the ball at the peak of your jump.

Picture 44

COMING DOWN

Greg Lee

Once you have caught the ball, it is important to come down in a good triple threat position. In Picture 45 you will see that Bill has the ball under his chin and is ready to start the new play. Don't throw your arms and elbows wildly; keep the ball under control.

Rebounding is a transition—the beginning of a new play. If you are on defense and get the ball, you are changing to offense, and it is on offense that your team can score.

Picture 45

chapter 14

Defense (Player with the Ball)

If basketball is half defense, then it stands to reason that defensive play is just as important as offensive play.

KEEP YOUR DISTANCE

Bill Walton

Good defense begins with a good triple threat position: chin up, weight balanced, and so on.

When you are guarding the player with the ball, it is important to maintain the correct distance from your opponent (Picture 46). If you are too far away, you cannot deny your opponent anything he wants to do, and if you are too close, he can drive around you.

Picture 46

79

To properly judge the correct distance, position yourself so that you can reach out with your near arm and touch your opponent's chest. If your opponent moves toward you, move back; if he moves away, you have to move toward him. Look at Picture 47 to see what I mean. My hand is right on the other player's chest, and I am ready to move with him in any direction.

Picture 47

While you are on defense, it is imperative that you never cross your feet. Use what we call the defensive slide. This doesn't mean jumping up and down. It simply means sliding your feet from one spot to another, as in Pictures 48 and 49. The head stays at the same level all the time so that you can see the court. Always maintain the proper distance from the player with the ball.

Picture 48   **Picture 49**

KNOW THE OPPONENT'S STRENGTHS

Greg Lee

When you are playing defense, it is important to know your opponent's strengths and weaknesses. Know whether he goes better to his right or to his left. As a rule, right-handers go better to the right, left-handers to the left. It is best to overplay about half a step in the direction of your opponent's strong side. This is illustrated in Picture 50. Can you see how Bill positions himself on the offensive player's right side? This will force the

Picture 50

Picture 51

offensive player to the weaker side, and Bill gets the advantage. By taking away the stronger side, you are forcing your opponent to go where he would rather not go.

Always keep your arms and elbows out; take up as much space as possible. If you have your arms and elbows down, it is easier for your opponent to drive past you. Should the offensive player get around you, you have to jump back into position. Never cross your feet. Don't turn and chase after the other player. You cannot play defense from behind the play, so you have to jump back between your opponent and the basket. In Picture 51 you can see how Bill jumped back to get between his opponent and the hoop.

chapter 15

Defending the Player without the Ball

One of the most important parts of playing defense is keeping the person you are guarding from getting the ball. Try to make your opponent take the ball in a position that is not comfortable.

GETTING INTO THE RIGHT POSITION

Bill Walton

Since only one player can have the ball at a time, you will find yourself during most of the game guarding a player without the ball. Your goal is to keep the ball away from your opponent.

Start in the normal defensive position; keep yourself between the ball and the person you are guarding, as in Picture 52. Keep your eyes on your opponent and the ball at all times. This sounds impossible, but there is a way to do it.

To know where your opponent is, touch him slightly with the hand that is away from the ball and keep your near arm up so that it blocks the passing lane. Picture 53 shows you the right way of doing this. By touching the other player, you can tell when he moves without actually having to look at him. By keeping your arm up, you are preventing the ball from coming directly to your opponent.

Picture 52

Picture 53

WATCH THE BACK DOOR

Greg Lee

It is very important not to get reversed or "back-doored" to the basket. If your opponent should get past you, you have to open up to the ball. Picture 54 shows you what I mean. Don't cross your feet. Pivot on your back foot so that you can see the ball and break up the play. This will take a lot of practice to master because the natural tendency is to turn toward the player you are defending, but if you do that, your back is to the ball, your opponent is ahead of you, and he is going to get the ball nearer the basket.

Picture 54

FORCE THE PLAY OUT

Bill Walton

When you are guarding the player without the ball, your main goal, aside from keeping your opponent from getting the ball, is to make him receive the ball as he is moving away from the basket, as in Picture 55. Obviously, if the offensive player is moving out from the hoop, it is going to be more difficult for him to score.

Picture 55

chapter 16

Playing against the Bigger, Slower Player

In a game you will find yourself playing against a bigger, slower, stronger player quite often, and it is important to know how to take advantage of your strengths to outplay your opponent.

CONTROL THE PLAY

Greg Lee

In a basketball game, chances are you will be matched with a player of your same general size. Guards are about equal with guards from the other team, forwards and centers

Picture 56

about the same. But as play progresses, you may find yourself up against a defender who towers over you (Picture 56). How do you deal with this situation?

The first thing you want to do is not let a bigger, stronger player muscle you up. Don't let your opponent control you; you should control your opponent. To do this make an inside pivot to force the player to back up so that you can use your quickness against him. Don't get pinned in. Notice in Picture 57 that the stronger player turned toward the defender and is forcing him into retreat.

Picture 57

FAKE THE DEFENDER

Bill Walton

The key is to get the bigger man moving because then you can beat him. Go one way; then come back the other. Make good fakes; make your opponent think you are going to drive past him. In Pictures 58 and 59 you see the player faking one way and then moving away in the other direction.

Picture 58

Picture 59

Remember to keep yourself in the triple threat position and move the ball around. If you leave it in one place, the defender is going to knock it out of your hand.

chapter 17

A Special Power Basic

Bill Walton

Basketball is an important part of my life, and I always try to play a game the best I possibly can. But the game, for me, doesn't start on the court; it begins well before the tip-off. I always try to visualize a game before I play it. I try to imagine what my opponent will do in certain situations and then plan a strategy that will counter his moves and give me the advantage.

Greg Lee

Concentration is very important. You always have to be aware of where the ball is, what your opponent is doing, where you need to be to protect the basket or to assist your teammate. Basketball is as much a mental game as it is a physical one, and you have to be on your toes constantly. Mental lapses mean mistakes.

Walt Hazzard

To play a good game, you have to be tough both mentally and physically. You have to be prepared for any situation, and you have to react quickly. To be successful, you have to master the fundamentals, perfect your technique, and play the game with every ounce of your soul.

chapter 18

A Power Basics Checklist

Rebounding

Assume the shot will be missed.
Start away from the basket and move toward it.
Most rebounds come to the opposite side from the shot.
Come down with the ball in the triple threat position.

Defending the player with the ball

Stay close to your opponent.
Be able to reach out and touch your opponent.
Never cross your feet—use the defensive slide.
Be aware of where your opponent may go.
If your opponent gets past you, jump back to regain
position.

Defending the player without the ball

Keep your opponent from getting the ball.
See man and ball.
Force your opponent to take ball in his most uncomfort-
able position.
If your opponent does get by you, open up to the ball.

Playing against the bigger, slower player

Keep the triple threat position.
Make the inside pivot to take advantage of your speed.
Make your opponent give ground.